Made in the USA
Las Vegas, NV
19 January 2024

84600922R10302